The Story of
Sarah McMurray

Copyright © 2024, 2025 by Isaac du Toit

Illustrations Copyright © Isaac du Toit

First published in Hardcover February 2024
Revised Edition in Paperback July 2025

Published by Isaac du Toit
Wellington, New Zealand

ISBN: 978-0-473-75467-9 (Paperback)

All rights reserved.

On August 26, 1848, in Nelson, New Zealand, a baby girl named Sarah was born into a large family. Her parents were Susannah Silcock (née Flower) and Captain Simon Bonnet Silcock, who was born in England and settled in Nelson in 1842 after bringing several shiploads of settlers to New Zealand.

In 1871, when Sarah was 23 years old, she married Robert McMurray. They moved to his farm in Brightwater, New Zealand.

Not long after, Robert acquired land in the densely forested Inangahua Valley, Westland. He went off to prepare for their new home. It took him two years to clear the land and build a house. During this time, Sarah carried on the work at the farm in Brightwater.

When Robert was finally ready for her, Sarah set off for Westport by ship. All she took with her was her household supplies, two pigs, and half a dozen chickens and ducks. Robert met her at the boat.

They then began a treacherous 50-mile journey up a narrow, muddy track through the dense forest. Sarah rode on horseback, while Robert walked beside her.

The supplies had to be transported up the Buller River, which was a risky endeavour due to the fierce rapids and falls.

Once Sarah had settled into her forest home, she had her hands very full. She had to make absolutely everything by hand. She rarely interacted with the outside world and had to endure months and months of rain. Sarah and Robert had six children, three of which were born during the time that they lived in the Inangahua Valley.

During her spare time, she took up woodworking, creating toys for her children and pieces of furniture to furnish her house.

She wrote in early February 1875:

"Dear Mother... We have such a nice place here, so quiet and comfortable... I have been here six months next Sunday and have only been away once...I began to think that you had all quite forgotten there were such people as us in the world."

Sarah and her family moved to the North Island in the 1880s, where they farmed at Awahuri. Later, they moved to Wanganui. As her family grew up and she had less farmwork to do, Sarah found time to pursue her growing passion for woodcarving. To improve her abilities in that artform, she enrolled in the local technical school.

Sarah was prolific and decorated her family's Wanganui home with a wealth of elaborately carved furnishings, such as mantelpieces, architraves, wardrobe doors and picture frames.

In 1914, Sarah and Robert retired to Palmerston North. Here, Sarah continued her woodcarving in the garden shed.

In a 1935 newspaper article, when Sarah was in her late 80s she said:

"My carving is done in a little workshop down in the garden. I am always happy down there, and if a piece of work interests me it is sometimes 11 p.m. before the anxious family can persuade me to go to bed."

Sarah died on September 14, 1943, in Palmerston North after a long life of 95 years. But her story and wood carvings survive unto the modern day, a testament to her skill and creativity.

Afterword

Sarah McMurray, c.1908 – photographer unknown

Sarah McMurray – date and photographer unknown

Sarah McMurray was a talented woodcarver during a period when the art form gained popularity among women in New Zealand.

From 1890 to 1910, woodcarving became a popular pastime for women, aligning with the Arts and Crafts movement that encouraged craftsmanship in everyday objects.

However many women's woodcarvings remain unattributed, leaving their talents largely unrecognised. Sarah represents a larger group of female woodcarvers who enriched New Zealand local craft during this time.

Sarah's interest in woodworking, however, seems to have taken root earlier. In Mary Menzies's diary, she recounts a trip her family took to the West Coast in 1883. During their journey, they stopped for breakfast at the home of Robert McMurray. Mary writes "*His wife we were told afterwards was a wonderful woman, for besides taking care of her house and children and making the best butter in the country she took to carpentering and sat up till twelve o'clock at night making furniture.*"

In Sarah's later years, her daughter Minnie became her helper and companion.

(Above Left) Close-up of a carved panel from a Kauri wardrobe, 1898 by Sarah McMurray. (Above Right) Close-up of an oak sideboard carved by Sarah McMurray for her granddaughter, Valerie, for her 21st birthday in July 1944. Sarah died prior to her completing the second drawer. Both in the collection of Marie Baird.

Griffin Table carved by Sarah McMurray.

Sources:
- The Book of New Zealand women – Ko kui ma te kaupapa / edited by Charlotte Macdonald, Merimeri Penfold and Bridget Williams. Wellington, Bridget Williams Books, 1991, Pages 392-394
- Manawatu Times, Volume 65, Issue 201, 26 August 1940, Page 5 https://paperspast.natlib.govt.nz/newspapers/MT19400826.2.33.4
- Manawatu Times, Volume 60, Issue 218, 16 September 1935, Page 6 https://paperspast.natlib.govt.nz/newspapers/MT19350916.2.39
- The Summer Book 2: A New Zealand Miscellany, Wellington, 1983 Page 108
- Sorzano, Rigel. 'Out of the woodwork', Auckland War Memorial Museum - Tāmaki Paenga Hira, Published: 11 11 2019

www.ingramcontent.com/pod-product-compliance
Lightning Source LLC
Chambersburg PA
CBRC092341290426
44109CB00009B/177